THE WORKBOOK:

Creating an offer your clients can't refuse

Activating the ICON effect

Stephanie Synclair

COPYRIGHT:

House of Icons Publishing, Las Vegas, Nevada

Copyright House of Icons LLC 2018

Published 2018

ISBN 978-1732104907

DISCLAIMER

To the dreamer who no longer wants to dream but is ready to do the work.
This is for you.

Introduction

2 years ago when I wrote the first book in this series, Shut Up and Do the Work, The entrepreneurs guide to creating massive success, it was a mindset book and mindset book only. That is all that I had in mind for it.

I'd spent my entire career building and completely reprogramming my mindset using the techniques given in that book. That was the core reason for my success. The 80/20 rule.

80% of the work I did was work on me. Getting rid of beliefs and belief systems that held me back from what I truly wanted to accomplish. 20% was on the action that needed to be taken. When I made the statement "do the work", that encompassed both of those. The mindset and the action.

I'd spent years reading others books all about work, work, work OR mindset, mindset, mindset. I rarely, if ever, heard anyone actually be honest and say that success takes both mindset and action. I wanted to be that different voice in the marketplace. I wanted to say what others aren't willing to say.

Since then, many of the entrepreneurs that you look up to, the Gary Vee's and Grant Cardone's have come out to admit the mindset work that they do. Because regardless of how much "go go go" you have, it won't be consistent if you haven't done the work on you.

Since the release of the original book I've read your emails, inboxes, DM's, reviews, etc and I've heard you. You want to now know WHAT to do business wise. I always knew that was only part 1 to the series. I just wasn't quite sure what the other parts would be. Almost two years later, I've realized that the series should be completed with the 5 ACTION steps after the mindset. Scratch that. The

ACTION steps as you're working on the mindset. Because, if you're anything like I was, I was to broke to only focus on the mindset before the action. They HAD to happen at the same time.

There is a 5 part system that I've taken all of my clients through whom I have worked with throughout the years. Each part of that system will become a new part in the Shut Up and Do the Work series and build upon each other so that you can go out and build your own successful company. It doesn't matter what industry you're in per say, but I will be talking from the view point of an expert entrepreneur. Everything I say can apply to any business.

Though the original book had a workbook section, this is a designated workbook. In all transparency, its a course, in book form. You're getting the EXACT information that I've given to clients over the last 9 years. Information that can completely change the inner workings of your business and help you generate millions. Take your time reading through the content and answering the questions. THIS IS FOR YOU even if you are a seasoned entrepreneur. As a matter of fact, I go through this quarterly to ensure I'm on track with the bigger goal at hand.

Are you ready?

Lets get into it!

The Big Mistake Most Entrepreneur's Make

In my almost 10 years of being a coach and mentor for entrepreneur's, I often see one BIG mistake that most make. They have this grand idea that lights them up. They believe that everyone will love it as much as they do, they package it and then they put it on the market. I too have fallen for my own ego with this one. And, I've heard other coaches teach this. "If you love it, they will too". Here's an easy piece of advice that will take you a long way...... THAT IS NOT NECESSARILY TRUE..... As a matter of fact, many of the things that light us up, those bright ideas, aren't necessarily the ideas that light our prospective clients up. They aren't what they feel they need.

The reality of this entrepreneurial world is knowing that we don't sell what we want to sell. We sell what our clients and customers want to buy. And if they don't want to buy it, even begrudgingly, we don't have a business.

So this may bring up the question to you, "Do we sell only what our clients want"? And that makes sense given the information that I just gave you. If what we want to sell isn't what they want to buy, then surely we should focus on what they want to buy right?! Nope! Not necessarily!

I know you may be thinking "Come on Stephanie, get to the point. I want to know" and I get it!!! But I want you to think about this for a moment. If you aren't selling what YOU want to sell them and you aren't selling them what THEY want, how do you figure out what you do need to sell them?

I'm going to make this easy for you.

Forget all that you want to sell.

Forget all that they want to buy (for now).

Get clear on what the FINAL result is that you offer.

This may be a feeling.. it usually is.

And that feeling then gets packaged into a product or an offering.

That is what you sell.

An outcome. A feeling. Thats it.

Let's Be Clear

You may now be asking why you bought this book because clearly I'm crazy right?!!? It may seem that way, but stay with me for a minute.

People don't buy things. They buy feelings, an experience or a result that gives them a certain feeling or experience.

Let's take Chanel. If you know me, you know that makes sense for me to use that as an example. I love Chanel. I love the Chanel brand. I love the story. All of it is perfection for me. No one wants to spend $5000 on a purse. No one wants to spend $1000 on jewelry that isn't 100% gold. Okay, I don't know this for a fact but I have a couple of Chanel pieces and their employees will tell you that it's a gold "formula" and just how much is actual gold, they can't tell you. That said, I am led to believe that it is not pure gold. So, why would anyone pay that for a "gold like" necklace or bracelet? I want you to really think about this for a moment before you move on reading. You can insert your favorite brand in place of Chanel if you aren't familiar with the brand but its important that you get clear on this within you. Why do YOU think anyone would pay the price that is paid for a leather purse? Or gold like jewelry?

Let's also take a look at the Hermes Birkin bag. On my podcast, Live Iconic, I talked about the Birkin Bag and how to get the Birkin experience within your business. I spoke about the fact that it is a rather basic leather bag, no extra detail, sometimes made with crocodile that starts at $20,000. The most expensive Birkin sold for $348,000 at an auction. Why would anyone, knowing how plain a Birkin is, pay the cost of a house, depending on where you live, for a basic leather bag?

The answer to both of those is the feeling you get while carrying, wearing and owning it. It is what it means to have one of those pieces. It is unspoken, but known. You walk with your head a little higher and a bit more confidence. Let's give credit where it is do, both these brands bags are handmade and superior quality. If a strap breaks you can take it back years later and have it repaired though I've never had one of my quality pieces tear in the least bit. If they did, I trust that it would be repaired. The fact is, the brands mean something. Even if most don't want to admit it.

That is because people invest in feelings.

PERIOD

The average entrepreneur doesn't create their business with this in mind. They create their business based off of need and most often what people need doesn't evoke their endorphins to going. Usually a need based buy isn't one that is talked about and shared with friends. Its also often the one bought last and done as cheaply as possible. With feelings based purchase, there is no limit to the amount that you can charge and that will be paid.

I wanted to start with this because it is so often overlooked. And the sales person… yeah you, (If you own a business or will be starting one, get used to hearing that.. you're a sales person. You have to sell you day in and day out.) that wins, that closes the most deals, makes the most money and changes the most lives is the person who can help their prospects understand that the feeling they are after comes from purchasing their product or service.

Cultivating the Ideal Experience

Now that you understand that feelings dominate the purchase decision of most people, it is imperative that you get clear on the feeling your program, product or service gives to your prospect.

Answer the following questions as honestly as you can. Remember, this is for you and to help you create a better product.

Based on the service or product category that you offer CURRENTLY, what is the dominant feeling that your ideal client has when they finish working with you? _____

What are your current offerings? If you sell products, such as in a boutique, list the category the product falls under. Example. If you have an e-commence store that sells cell phone cases, chargers, batteries, cell phones, key chains and other novelty items, your list may look something like 1. Cell Phone accessories 2. Beauty Products 3. Luxury Novelty items, etc. In one of my personal e-commerce stores, we sell novelty dog items so my list would be. 1. Dog Clothes 2. Dog Accessories. If you're a service based business, such as a hair stylist, your list may look something like, 1. Hair Extensions 2. Signature Hair Care Products This means that your list will look differently depending on your industry.

List your current offerings below:

1.

2.

3.

4.

5.

Based upon those CURRENT offerings, what is the feeling that your client or customer has when they purchase your current offerings?

Offering:	Feeling they leave with:
1.	1.
2.	2.
3.	3.
4.	4.
5.	5.

This next question is just as important in the self coaching process.

How do you know that is the feeling that your clients/customers leave with when they purchase from you?

_____

_____

_____

It is imperative that you're as honest with yourself as possible here. This exercise works to help you get clear on why you may not be selling as much as you could of your offering.

I remember the first time I took one of my clients through this part of the assessment. Initially, they kept inserting the feeling they HOPED the client/customer would leave with. We didn't exactly pin that down until we reached the question of "how do you know" and it always came back to "That is what I THINK they are leaving with".

This isn't a place you want to "think" but rather a place you want to know, for sure, that you're clients are leaving feeling this way about your product. When we got super clear on the feeling her customers felt, she quickly realized that her clients weren't that excited to buy. They only came to her when they were at their wits end; when they had no other options.

That isn't what she wanted though. She wanted her customers to be thrilled to work with her. She wanted them to be excited to go through the process, excited to implement and excited to tell their friends about her offerings. She realized that she wasn't attracting all the clients she could because there was no gratification up front from working with her.

Let's go back to a luxury purse example. I will use myself here. I remember the first time I bought a high end designer brand. I'd worked really hard and I'd made a certain dollar amount that month and to reward myself I was going to go buy a nice leather bag that could be stylish that year and 20 years from then. A piece that I could pass on to my granddaughter. I remember getting up that Thursday with a price point in mind. $2,000. Now, I know in the grand scheme of thing on the luxury purse scale, that is not the highest but I hadn't paid more than $500 for a handbag at this point so $2,000 felt like "I'd arrived". I did a ton of research before I left and based on my price point and the style I desired, I decided that the Alexander McQueen Large Padlock Tote would likely be what I'd get. I didn't want to order online as I wanted a lux in store experience. If I remember correctly, it came to about $2300, just above my price point but I was in love with it. It was a tan bag, big enough to carry my laptop if need be, but not so big that it looked like a suitcase. It was a bag that I knew would forever be stylish. You know how a lot of Jackie O style is still in today? That is the look I was going for, on a larger scale. Saying "yes" to that bag, I felt accomplished. I knew that I'd crossed another level. You see, I wasn't going into debt to buy it, to keep up with anyone else, or anything of the sort. I could really afford it. For me, it signified a different phase in my life and in my business. A phase where luxury purchases were a norm. I carried that bag with so much pride that season. No one knew but me what that purse signified but that feeling I now associate forever with Alexander McQueen or any other luxury bag for that matter. I don't buy "expensive" purses for the name. I buy them for the feeling that I get because I can buy them. The feeling of accomplishment.

Stop for a moment and think back to a time in your life where you bought something or signed up for something that you were really excited about. Think over the process that you went through, the full experience. This isn't about price. You can have the same amazing experience with something $50. Just think back on how you felt.

Thinking back on that, what was your experience? What were you buying and why?

_____

_____

_____

_____

_____

_____

_____

_____

What did you FEEL when you made that purchase or investment?

(Remember as I discussed the purse, I felt a feeling of *accomplishment* with that purchase)

_____

_____

_____

_____

_____

_____

Now, talking a look at a program, product or service that you've invested in and remembering the feeling that you felt when you purchased, does your offering do the same or similar for your target clients?

This is the point when most people began to realize that though they offer something amazing, people aren't excited about buying it because there is no reason to be.

You see, most businesses follow this format in order to create new offers.

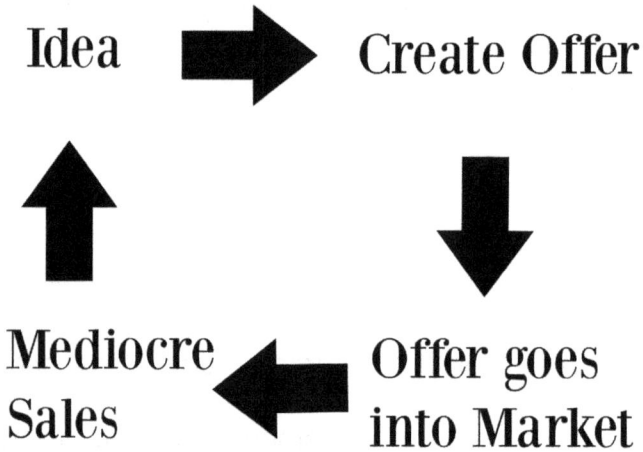

The process starts off with the "idea". Now this idea can be a product, a service.. it doesn't really matter. It's usually the thing that you're going to sell. They then create an offer for it. The offer includes a few pictures usually or if you're selling a service, the "copy" around the offer. This for many if you're in the expert industry would be the "sales page". If you have an online store it would be the images related to your product that you're selling. You would then hit "live" on it and open it to the public. You'll talk about it on social media, in ads, maybe even mainstream media and you would lead people to the buy page. After you've exhausted your sales there, you move on to the next "idea" and the process starts over again. For years, this process has worked… and pretty well. But in the last 2-3 years we have seen more people than ever before with online businesses. That means more people selling the same product or service.

Now, you may sit back and think "no one sells what I sell". I am here to tell you, no matter how different you think what you offer is, it's probably not that different. Unless you're creating cutting edge new technologies, inventions, etc, what you're doing has been done. And that means its a lot of noise within the marketplace that you're selling in. People comparison shop for everything. And those we assume they shop for the "cheapest" (and some do but they're likely not our clients), most shop for the thing that stands out to them.

This creates a problem when everyone sells the same thing in different colors, sizes, styles, etc. Or even in a service industry, unless you've positioned yourself at the top in a way that you are seen as the "go to", above everyone else, they're checking out multiple people who do exactly what you do. And the thing that is going to sway them is the "feeling" aspect that we just spoke about.

In order for your product, service, offering to stand out, above the crowd, you must implement what I like to call the ICON EFFECT into your business. It is the same thing that brands such as Birkin and Chanel have tapped into in order to have customers on lists for YEARS to spend some peoples yearly salary on a handbag.

If you haven't figured it out yet, the ICON effect can also be called the "feeling" effect and in the simplest terms possible, it's consciously activating an effect within your offering that gives your ideal audience excitement about purchasing.

The KEY term here is conscious. You must consciously cultivate this effect. It doesn't happen by chance and this will be very important to keep in mind as we move forward.

Thinking over your own purchases, investments, etc that you were totally lit up and excited about, or even some that you want to make in the future, what is the feeling that you really want to bring up and out of your clients when they find out about what you offer? Remember, this is BEFORE they actually buy.

I personally am sitting and dreaming of the day when I can buy an amazing Italian Villa overlooking the Mediterranean. It is a realtor that I follow on Instagram who covers Italian properties and I sit and dream quite often when I have free time. It started out as a cute "idea" and the more I looked at pictures and thought about it, and read more stories of people who bought dream properties, picked up and move, the more realistic it became to me. So, I am actively putting things in place to make that happen. The excitement of the journey to reach the goal is probably just as exciting as attaining the goal. For me, this accomplishment will signify freedom which is extremely important to me. When the right home shows up, at the right price, at the right time, no one will have to convince me to buy. My mind is set and I am definitely buying because I am caught up in the dream. I've seen myself living in the house, cooking in the kitchen, swimming in the pool, grabbing lemons off the lemon tree in the yard… I have already become invested in this outcome AND I HAVEN'T EVEN FOUND THE HOME YET.

Most of us have, or have had situations where there have been things we've wanted and we coveted them even before we actually purchased them. Now, imagine this is your prospective client. What is the feeling that you really want to bring up and out of your clients when they find out about what you offer?

_____

_____

_____

_____

_____

_____

Does your CURRENT offer create this feeling in your prospective clients? The answer here is usually no because most people without big marketing departments, never actually think about this.

Earlier I showed you the flow of most business owners as they create new programs, products and services to offer. The following flow chart is one that I would suggest for the person looking to activate the ICON Effect within their business.

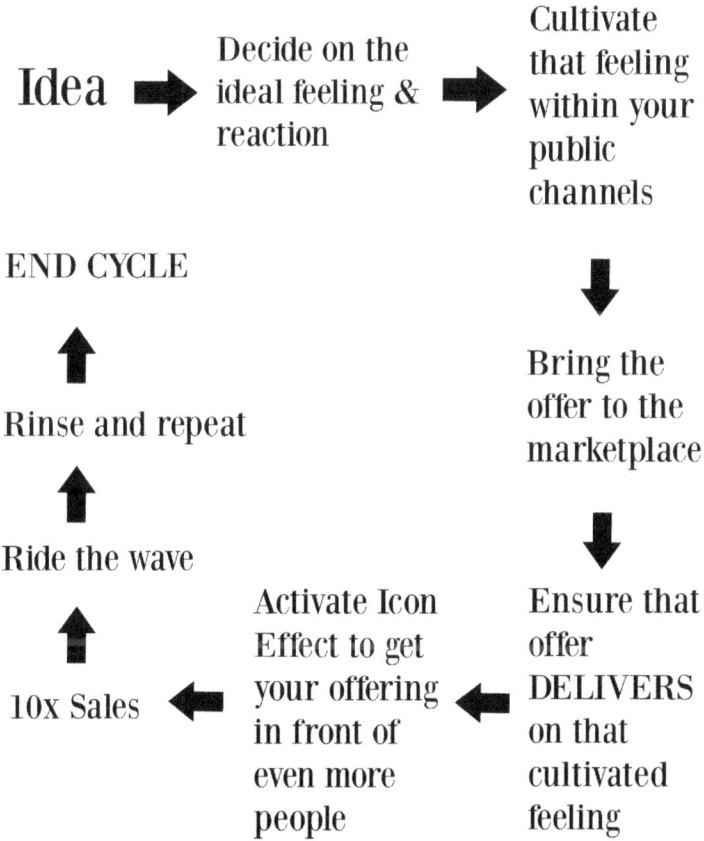

Idea ➡ Decide on the ideal feeling & reaction ➡ Cultivate that feeling within your public channels

⬇

Bring the offer to the marketplace

⬇

END CYCLE

⬆

Rinse and repeat

⬆

Ride the wave

⬆

10x Sales ⬅ Activate Icon Effect to get your offering in front of even more people ⬅ Ensure that offer DELIVERS on that cultivated feeling

1. The process always starts with the idea. No matter what system you're using, everything in life begins with an idea or a thought. Of course its important that you ensure your idea for a program, product, service, offering, etc is actually something that people actually want. I tend to trust you, as the expert on what you offer and on your client knows exactly what this is already and wouldn't create anything that didn't fit that.

2. The next step is to decide on the feeling that you'd like prospects to get before they buy…the lead up that ensures that when it is available, it is an immediate yes for them.

3. This is where many people miss out. Even if they have thought about a specific feeling that they'd like their clients and customers to have, they

haven't thought about the pre-purchase and they haven't quite thought about how that is going to translate in their marketing before the prospect buys. I will be going in depth on this in the next workbook which is solely dedicated to marketing this offer that clients can't refuse because it doesn't really matter how amazing the offer is if no one know it exists. If you're already a beast at marketing, you can go ahead and get started even if you don't yet have the marketing workbook but it is imperative that you use public platforms such as social media to help get the "feeling" out before the product is available for purchase. How do you do that? In the simplest terms and without writing out the entire marketing manual within this workbook, it is starting somewhat of a movement. Taking advantage of custom hashtags for your offering and using them across platforms. Its creating branded products, regular videos, pictures, etc. Its creating an effect that whatever is coming is something that need not be missed. A club or sorority of sorts that is the hottest thing popping and they will regret not jumping on board when time comes. It is the "set up" to the offer.

4. At this point you bring your offer to the public. The sales page goes live, the buy now button pops up and you await your orders while still having step 3 live and in action.

5. THIS IS JUST AS IMPORTANT AS THE IDEA ITSELF. You must ensure that when your clients and customers say yes and hit that buy button, the product itself actually meets the anticipation that you created before they bought. This is where universal branding comes in, custom packaging, customer service experiences like no

other, questions answered before they have to ask, etc. The "rah rah" that they felt before they purchased should be the same thing they feel when they receive that package in the mail, that email with the download, that phone call from your team, etc. This is a HUGE part of the continued success.

6. At this point, the Icon Effect is live and well and you're stepping it up using the Icon Effect Marketing strategies in workbook 2. Selling your product is not the end of the sales cycle or the Icon Effect. Because you see, you want to use your sales to create more sales and to create somewhat of a viral effect for your offering. Where MANY MANY MANY people slip up is assuming the sale is the end. You want a couple of things to happen when your clients and customers purchase from you. First, you want

your customer to want to purchase from you again and again and again. (Workbook 5 will go deep into client and customer retention). If your client purchases stop at one thing, you haven't done your job. First, depending on your business, I am sure there was more that your client needed that you weren't able to provide and second you can't allow your business to be a hit'em and quit'em. Next on top of wanting repeat clients and customers, it is imperative that your clients purchase generates more purchases from other people. This happens 2 ways, again both ways detailed in the marketing manual. The first way is from the initial sale and the excitement from that itself and the second way is from the testimonial or result after client or customer has had and used your program, product and service for some amount of time.

7. Using these strategies you re-activate the icon effect and boost sales 10x the initially one. It is like having a small army of people who love you, what you talk about, your offerings, etc so much that they HAVE to tell everyone they know and your little army begins to grow…and fast.

8. From there you realize that a huge wave has formed, even if you don't consciously promote daily, sales are still coming in. But this is important… DON'T STOP. Even though it is a wave, eventually if there is no momentum, the wave will slow down and level out.

9. Rinse and repeat these strategies having clients and customers constantly coming back for more.

10. I am adding an additional one here that wasn't in the original cycle but needs to be said. I alluded to this earlier but there is always something else that you can create to serve your clients and

customers even more. When you're done with the cycle, you rinse and repeat for new clients and customers but there is always something else that your current clients need. In workbook 5 I will be going in depth on what that is, how to create it, etc so be on the lookout.

Tying it all up

I hope that the main thing that you've gotten is that it actually doesn't matter as much what you sell than how that thing makes those buying it feel. From what it is, to the marketing of it, to actually getting access to the thing that is purchased. That is what matters in creating an offer that is impossible to pass up.

I've been on this "healthy" journey for quite a while. I start and stop and start and stop. Recently, I purchased a set of products that speed up metabolism, increase energy, etc. I'd seen it on social media for a while and people where so excited about it that it made me excited. What's the miracle about this product? What's so good about it? I jumped online and ordered the set. It was roughly $300 which isn't a big deal if it does what it said its going to do but what really shocked me is when I got it home, looked at the ingredients and realized I could have bought all of it for under $40. Now, I have insight here where others may not simply because I used to own an all natural spa which included metabolism support products. This kit which was $300 included a bottle of green coffee bean pills, a bottle of HCG and a bottle of B12. I laughed so hard when I saw it because I realized I'd fallen for my own Icon Effect. You see, it's not the actual products, it's the feeling that being apart of the group that purchases gets to be apart of. Her kit sells out in a couple of hours so it creates this scarcity effect. People are always posting their results which are amazing (The diet that's included is basically the Keto diet so weight loss would totally make sense) and she creates these "groups" for monthly health challenges. So what I bought was really the community that she created of women supporting others on this journey.

Now, if I weren't armed with my business knowledge I'd probably be a bit pissed off. In actuality, I was impressed. I was caught up in the Icon Effect of the offer and the Icon Effect Cycle listed in the previous pages. And this girl is doing well over a million with these products that are easily accessible and cheap and that she branded. You see, there is nothing amazing about any of the products. Her offer is what is amazing. Her positioning. And that's what I was really buying.

I told you this story because with the right offer positioned correctly based on the "feelings" that your product evoke, can get even the most experienced person such as myself to buy what you offer.

Now in her defense, almost every over the counter supplement is simple like these. She just used brilliant and effective offer techniques.

Now, I want you to think about your current offer or product or service. How can you make it better? The thing that it promises, the way it makes your client/customer feel, how can that get better.

I have actually created a FREE program that goes along with this workbook that walks you through this entire process. Let's create or re-create your program, TOGETHER. Head to www.ShutUpAndDoTheWork.com/WKB1Course to get immediate access to the video course.

Keep In Touch

I'd love to hear your thoughts on the workbook.
Please be sure to post your review on Amazon and
be sure to tag your photos on Instagram with
#SUDTW

Find me on Instagram at instagram.com/
StephanieSynclair
Facebook at facebook.com/
StephanieTheMarketingMaven
Listen to my podcast, Live Iconic on Itunes, Google
Play, Spotify and iHeart Radio

www.ingramcontent.com/pod-product-compliance
Lightning Source LLC
Chambersburg PA
CBHW071124210326
41519CB00020B/6410